Where Animals Live

The World of Bats

Words by Virginia Harrison

Adapted from Helen Riley's *The Bat in the Cave*

Photographs by
Oxford Scientific Films

Gareth Stevens Publishing
Milwaukee

Contents

Note: The use of a capital letter for a bat's name means that it is a specific type, or *species*, of bat (for example, Noctule Bat). The use of a lowercase, or small, letter means that it is a member of a larger *group* of bats.

Bats and Their Homes

Bats are the only mammals that can fly. Their scientific name is *Chiroptera* (ki-ROP-ter-ah), which means "hand-wing." Their wings are made of stretchy skin pulled across long fingers.

Unlike us, bats are *nocturnal*. They sleep hanging upside-down during the day, and they wake up when the Sun sets. At night, bats fly out of their caves in search of food. The Long-fingered Bats shown above are in a typical cluster in their *roost*.

3

Bats Around the World

Bats live almost everywhere in the world. There are about 950 *species* of bats divided into two main groups: *Megachiroptera* ("big hand-wing") and *Microchiroptera* ("small hand-wing").

Megachiroptera, or "megabats," have large eyes and long noses. These Egyptian Fruit Bats (below) are a good example of the megabat. Usually feeding on fruit, megabats live in *tropical* regions. The biggest megabats have a wingspan of up to 5 feet (1.5 m). They are about the size of a chicken — with very long wings!

Most bats are Microchiroptera, or "microbats."
Except for the polar regions and other remote
places, microbats are everywhere. Microbats
like this Noctule (above) are the size and shape
of mice, with 18-inch (50-cm) wingspans.

Within both bat groups, males and females are
about the same size, shape, and color (below).

Finding a Way in the Dark

The tiny eyes of this microbat (called a Naked-backed Bat) are not much help in the dark, so it must find its way with *echolocation*. Microbats produce high-pitched *ultrasonic* noises. These noises bounce off objects, and the bats use the echoes to judge the size, distance, and movement of everything in their path.

Many microbats, like the Brown Long-eared Bat, have big ears and a flap of skin called a tragus that may help the bat track the direction of the echoes.

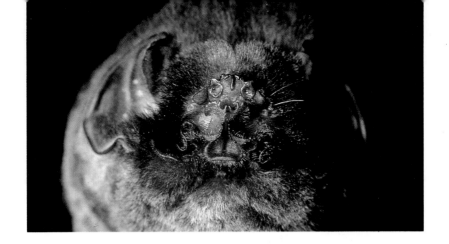

To help them echolocate, some microbats have odd-shaped faces. For example, the Leaf-chinned Bat shown above has extra skin flaps on its ears and nose. These flaps help bats make their ultrasonic noises.

The only megabat species that can echolocate is the Rousette Fruit Bat. It produces nonultrasonic clicking noises that echo off cave walls. Once this bat is outside its dark roost, it uses its eyes to find its way.

The body of a bat

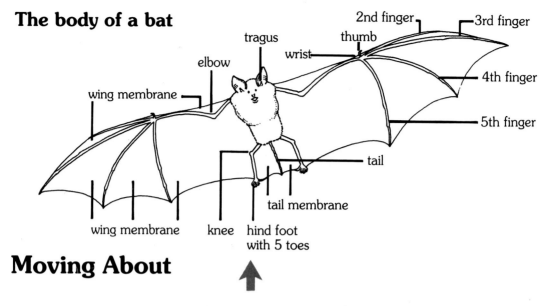

2nd finger

3rd finger

thumb

tragus

wrist

elbow

4th finger

wing membrane

5th finger

tail

wing membrane   knee   hind foot
with 5 toes

tail membrane

Moving About

Bats' bodies seem small when compared to their forelimbs. The bones of their fingers are very long and act as supports to the wing, with its thin skin stretching from the bat's side, back, and legs.

Bats are designed for a flying and hanging way of life, so on the ground, most bats are not quite as skillful as they are up in the air. The Common Vampire Bat, however, is an agile crawler and leaper.

When bats hang in their roosts, the five claws of their back feet grip tightly to the roof — even when they are asleep!

Generally, bats fly the same way as birds. But bats must be able to change direction quickly in the darkness of night. So they must fly more slowly and carefully than birds.

Bats vary in their flying ability and in the shape of their wings. Greater Horseshoe Bats have short, broad wings with which they fly slowly and skillfully. In contrast, Mexican Free-tailed Bats and other fast-flying bats have wings that are long and narrow.

Feeding on Animals ⬆

This Greater Horseshoe Bat is about to catch a moth. Like the Pipistrelle Bat (shown at right), it is *insectivorous* and has sharp teeth for cutting through the tough skin of its insect *prey*. ➡

Most bats are insectivorous. You may see them swooping and dodging in the air as they use echolocation to follow their prey. Bats usually catch prey in their mouths, but they may also use the skin flap between their legs to scoop up a struggling insect. Bats can also pluck insects off plants or the surface of a pond.

Vampire bats of South America get their name from the fact that they feed on blood. The Common Vampire Bat drinks the blood of farm animals. Its saliva has a special substance in it that keeps the victim's blood from clotting. The bat can then take out half its own weight in blood. This does not harm the animal, but the danger may be in rabies and other diseases that bats often carry.

As you might guess, the Fisherman's Bat (lower right) catches and eats fish. It uses echolocation to detect ripples on the water's surface. It then swoops down and grasps the fish with the sharp, curved claws on its hind feet.

Feeding on Plants

Many bats from Africa, Latin America, and other tropical areas eat the flowers and fruit of plants. These bats live in tropical areas because plants grow all year round in the warm climate.

The Little Fruit-eating Bat (above) is one example of a *frugivorous* (fru-GIV-er-us) bat. It prefers soft, ripe fruits that it can easily crush between its blunt teeth. It swallows the fruit juices and spits out the flesh.

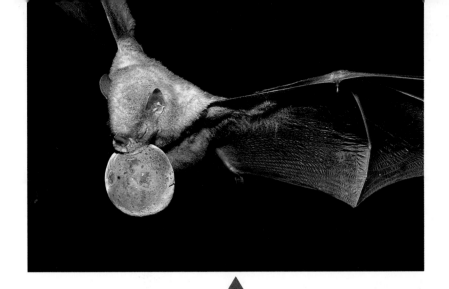

↑

This Spear-nosed Bat is carrying a fig away from a fig tree. Bats spread seeds around when they eat, so fruit trees benefit from the bats' feeding.

Like bees, some bats feed on *pollen* and nectar and thus *pollinate* flowers. Pollen that sticks to the bats' fur may be accidentally carried from one flower to another. These bats have long tongues with bristly ends that can reach down into flowers and lap up nectar. The yellow dust on the fur of this Mexican Long-nosed Bat is pollen.

↓

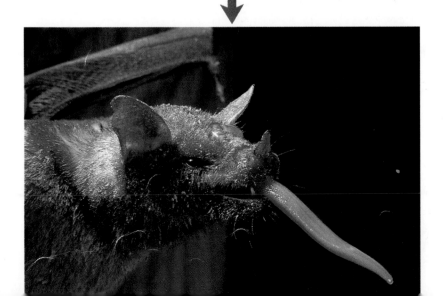

Surviving the Winter ▲

This Daubenton's Bat is in *hibernation*. It has allowed its body temperature to cool down almost as low as the temperature of the air around it. Bats hibernate in cool, damp places and are often covered with drops of water.

Hibernating bats may hang spaced apart, like these Lesser Horseshoe Bats (above). Or they may cluster together, like these Indiana Bats (left).

Only bats that live in *temperate* climates need to hibernate. When the weather turns cold, flying insects are scarce, so the bats need to live off their bodies' fat reserves.

To conserve body fluids, bats hibernate in humid caves. Hibernating bats take at least half an hour to wake up fully. So they must also choose a place where *predators* can't find them.

Horseshoe bats, like the Lesser Horseshoe,
wrap their wings around their bodies during
hibernation. But most bats, like this Natterer's
Bat (right), fold their wings while hibernating.
This is how they avoid the loss of body fluid
from large areas of naked skin.

In North America and Europe, bats enter
caves to hibernate in September or October.
Throughout their hibernation, they awake at
intervals and may fly in search of food. But
they don't stop hibernating until April or May.

Some bats, like the Brown Long-eared Bat and the Barbastelle, only hibernate in caves when the weather gets really cold. For the rest of the winter, they hibernate in trees, where they move into hollows in the trunk or crevices in the bark.

Hibernating bats should not be awakened before they are ready, as they use up lots of their stored fat in the process of waking up. If they cannot find food to replace their lost energy, they will die.

The Breeding Season

Below: a year in the life of the Greater Horseshoe Bat (shown opposite). Bats that live in temperate areas of the world, like this one, are only fully active for about five months a year, during the spring and summer. Each female bat has just enough time to give birth and raise her young.

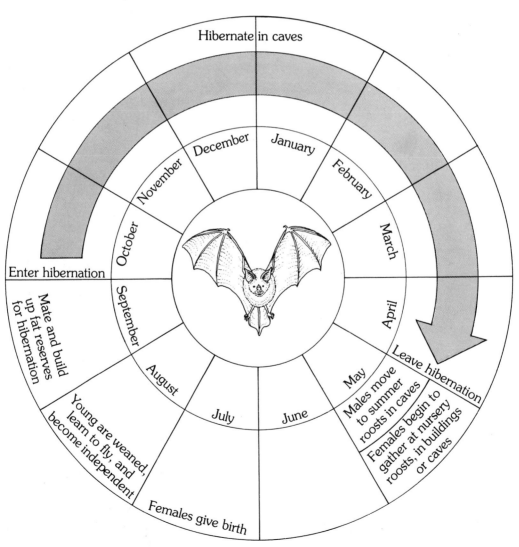

Hibernate in caves

December
November
January
October
February
March
Enter hibernation
September
April
Mate and build up fat reserves for hibernation
May
Males move to summer roosts in caves
Leave hibernation
August
Females begin to gather at nursery roosts, in buildings or caves
Young are weaned, learn to fly, and become independent
July
June
Females give birth

Bats must mate in the fall so the *embryo* bats can begin developing as soon as the female emerges from hibernation. The male's sperm may be stored in the female's *uterus* while she hibernates, ready to fertilize the eggs she will produce in the spring. Or the eggs may be fertilized soon after mating and remain undeveloped until spring.

In the tropics, rain means food. So rain, not cold weather, has the most influence on when bats breed. Bats arrange their breeding seasons so they give birth when food is plentiful.

Mating and Giving Birth

Like most bats, these Leaf-chinned Bats will not stay together after they have mated. The father does not help raise the baby bats. In fact, he will leave to mate with other females.

Female bats of the same species gather in nursery colonies to give birth to and raise their young. ➡

The colonies often gather in caves. Roof spaces in houses are also popular because they get warmer than caves in summer. And the warmer the baby bats are, the faster they grow!

Bats give birth to only one or two babies per litter. Any more would weigh them down and make flying very difficult.

Growing Up

Baby bats are born naked and blind, but not entirely helpless. They have strong hind feet so they can cling to their mother or to the roof of the roost.

Baby bats are also born with milk teeth, which allow them to suckle right away. These suckling Gould's Long-eared Bats (lower left) are seven days old. ⬇

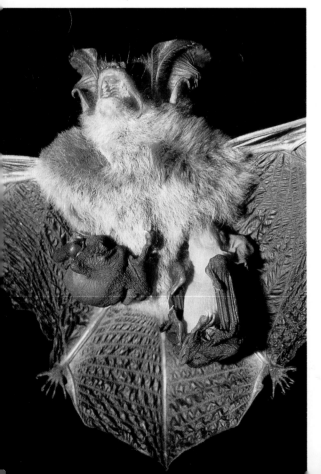

These Little Brown Bats are a week old. But they are already nearly as big as their mother!

Baby bats from each nursery huddle together while their mothers find food. The mother of this nearly grown Brown Long-eared Bat has returned to give it warmth and protection.

The young of small species of bats develop quickly. It usually takes from six weeks to two months for them to grow into adults. They usually take their first flight at the age of three weeks to a month. At this point, they are *weaned*, and permanent teeth have replaced their milk teeth. Babies of larger bats take longer to develop. They may be three months old before they take their first flight.

Bats, Birds, and Other Cave Dwellers

The barrenness of caves discourages most life forms from living in them. There is so little light that green plants cannot grow.

But a special cave food chain exists in some large tropical caves. These caves may have thousands of bats living in them! In these caves, bat *guano* accumulates in large amounts. Many tiny creatures — like these beetle larvae — live and feed in the guano (below).

These tiny creatures are eaten by larger creatures, such as spiders, centipedes, and snakes.

Few animals depend on caves the way bats do. One animal that has a "batty" way of life is the Oilbird of South America (opposite). It roosts in a cave by day and uses a form of echolocation while in the dark depths of the cave. By night, it flies through the tropics in search of oily fruits and nuts.

Threats to Bats

Few animals feed on bats. Bats sleep hidden in caves and fly in the dark of night, so they are not easily caught. The Barn Owl (below) and other birds of prey will kill a bat if they have a chance, and weasels and snakes may crawl into a bat roost to find a meal.

The bat's main enemy, though, is people.

↑

Bats have long been portrayed as wicked in books and pictures (above). This negative image does not help bats, since so many farmers and homeowners also consider them pests.

People use poisons to kill bats, thus reducing the numbers of some rarer bat species. People also destroy the bat's environment in many ways. For example, many bat *habitats* are ruined when people clear forests to provide land for farms and towns. Humans also disturb bats' roosting places by exploring — and polluting — caves.

Sadly, many people treat bats cruelly out of fear and misunderstanding. In the past, the figure of a bat could bring beauty to a goblet like the one shown below. But it could also be used to create an eerie feeling, as in the engraving above, or to suggest evil figures like the devil or Dracula.

In many countries, bats are now protected by law and by groups of concerned people. These people provide extra homes for tree-dwelling bats (above). They also cover cave entrances with grating through which bats can go, but people cannot.

Life in the Cave

This food chain is found only in large caves where lots of bats live. It is based on something only the bats can provide — their guano.

Food Chain

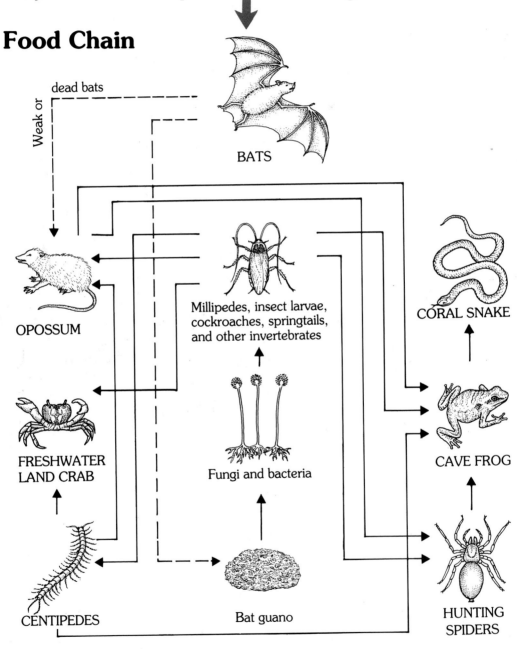

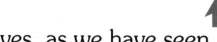

Caves, as we have seen, are used by most bat species at some time in their lives.

Bats and their habitats are now protected in many countries. But we need to learn more about bats in order to further understand and protect these furry, flying creatures.

Index and New Words About Bats

These new words about bats appear in the text on the pages shown after each definition. Each new word first appears in the text in *italics*, just as it appears here.

Reading level analysis: SPACHE 2.6, FRY 3, FLESCH 91 (very easy), RAYGOR 4, FOG 3

Library of Congress Cataloging-in-Publication Data

Harrison, Virginia, 1966-

    The world of bats / words by Virginia Harrison ; adapted from Helen Riley's The bat in the cave ; photographs by Oxford Scientific Films.

        p.   cm. — (Where animals live)

    Summary: Simple text and illustrations depict the lives of bats in their natural setting describing how they feed, defend themselves, and breed.

    ISBN 0-8368-0137-7

    1. Bats—Juvenile literature. [1. Bats.] I. Riley, Helen. Bat in the cave. II. Oxford Scientific Films. III. Title. IV. Series.

QL737.C5H37   1989

599.4—dc20   89-4471

The authors and publishers wish to thank the following for permission to reproduce copyright material: **Oxford Scientific Films Ltd.** for front cover, pp. 8 and 10 (Stephen Dalton); pp. 2, 13 below, and 25 (J. A. L. Cooke); p. 3 (C. and D. Broomhall); p. 4 (Anthony Bannister); title page, p. 5 above, 22 right, 29, and 31 (Alastair Shay); back cover, pp. 5 below and 22 left (Kathie Atkinson); pp. 6 and 12 (Richard Laval); p. 7 above (Robert W. Mitchell); pp. 7 below and 21 below (Press-tige Pictures); pp. 9, 11 left, 14 above, 15, 16, 17, 19, 21 above (Richard Packwood); p. 11 right (Partridge Films Ltd.); p. 13 above (David Thompson); p. 14 below (Lynn M. Stone); p. 20 (Raymond A. Mendez); p. 23 (E. R. Degginger); p. 24 above (M. P. L. Fogden); p. 24 below (G. I. Bernard); p. 26 (Mark Hamblin). Mary Evans Picture Library for p. 28 above, and C. F. L. Giraudon, Paris, for p. 28 below. Page 27 courtesy of Ben Gaskell.

Printed in the United States of America

1 2 3 4 5 6 7 8 9 95 94 93 92 91 90 89

For a free color catalog describing Gareth Stevens' list of high-quality children's books call 1 (800) 433-0942